AF527061

RightQ

The Right Question

Unlocking a Life of Clarity and Purpose

" Right **Questions** *are the* **keys** to unlocking life's ***mysteries*** and discovering the ***treasures*** *within."*

By Abdullah Khan

In the Name of Allah, The Most Gracious, The Most Merciful

All praise is due to Allah (Glorified & Exalted), who granted us the mind to think, the heart to feel, and the will to seek truth. May this work serve as a means to inspire reflection, foster growth, and align with the ultimate purpose of our existence.

Dedication

To those seeking clarity amidst life's chaos,
To the dreamers who dare to imagine new possibilities,
To the resilient souls who rise after every fall,
And to the seekers of truth and purpose,
May these pages guide you toward clarity, fulfillment, and self-discovery.

This book is for you, with heartfelt gratitude and belief in your potential.

Acknowledgments

This book would not have been possible without the support, inspiration, and guidance of countless individuals.

I extend my deepest gratitude to:

- **My family**, for their unwavering encouragement and belief in my vision.
- **The great scholars**, past and present, whose timeless wisdom enriches this work.
- **My teachers**, who inspire and challenge me to strive for excellence.
- **My friends**, whose companionship and insights enriched this journey.
- **Readers like you**, whose curiosity and commitment to personal growth motivate this work.

Above all, I thank Allah, The Most Merciful, whose guidance and blessings have illuminated this journey.

Copyright and Publication Information

Book Title: The Right Question: Unlocking a Life of Clarity and Purpose

Author: Abdullah Khan

ISBN: 978-93-342-1762-9

For permission requests and inquiries, please contact:
abdullah.khan@live.in

Legal Disclaimer and Notice

This book is intended as a resource for personal growth, self-improvement, and intentional living. The concepts and methods discussed herein, including RightQs, are based on the author's research, understanding, and personal insights. While every effort has been made to ensure accuracy, the content is not a substitute for professional advice, including but not limited to medical, psychological, legal, or financial consultation.

The case studies and examples included in this book are fictional and are intended solely for illustrative purposes. Any resemblance to actual individuals, living or deceased, or real-life situations is purely coincidental. These examples are crafted to demonstrate the principles and concepts discussed, and their outcomes may vary for readers depending on personal circumstances.

Reader Responsibility:

The practices and tools outlined in this book are intended for personal reflection and growth. They do not replace or modify the established acts of worship (*'Ibadah*) as prescribed in Islam or any other religious obligations. This book aims to complement, not substitute, spiritual and professional guidance.

Readers are encouraged to consult qualified professionals for specific concerns related to health, finance, or legal matters.

The author and publisher expressly disclaim any liability for direct or indirect losses, damages, or harm resulting from the application of the concepts or practices described in this book. Your decisions, actions, and results are your sole responsibility.

CONTENTS

PREFACE

Welcome to the Journey

Imagine standing at the edge of a vast forest, its paths shrouded in mystery. You feel a pull toward discovery, but the way forward isn't clear. This forest mirrors life—its uncertainties, challenges, and infinite possibilities.

Let me share the story of Amal, an architect who once found herself lost—not in a physical sense, but in her sense of purpose. She felt overwhelmed by career demands and longed for work that aligned with her values. One day, she began asking herself a transformative question: **"What small step can I take today to create the life I truly desire?"**

This simple inquiry became her guiding light. Within months, Amal reconnected with her passion for sustainable design, started mentoring young professionals, and built a career that aligned with her deepest values.

Like Amal, we all possess the power to rewrite our stories. This book is your guide to asking transformative questions — the **RightQs** — that illuminate your path, cultivate resilience, and inspire growth. Together, let's embark on a journey to uncover clarity, purpose, and the strength to thrive.

Why This Book Matters

In today's fast-paced and distraction-filled world, clarity and purpose often feel elusive. The complexity of modern life demands tools that help us pause, reflect, and realign our actions with our values. This book offers those tools, presenting a practical framework grounded in timeless wisdom and tailored for a global audience.

Imagine navigating a busy intersection, overwhelmed by the noise and confusion. Without a clear map, it's easy to feel lost. This book serves as your map, guiding you through the chaos of daily life and helping you make intentional, purposeful decisions.

Each chapter provides insights and strategies to:

- Reconnect with your values and priorities.
- Navigate challenges with resilience and clarity.
- Rediscover joy and fulfillment in your daily life.

This book matters because it empowers you to take control of your journey and create a life that reflects your true essence.

What This Book Offers

This book is designed to be more than a collection of ideas—it is a practical guide that empowers you to transform your life. By mastering the art of RightQs, you will discover the clarity, resilience, and purpose needed to navigate life's complexities.

Key Features of This Book:

1. **Practical Integration of RightQs**: Transformative questions guide reflection and action, enabling you to craft personalized solutions for your unique challenges.
2. **Blend of Timeless Wisdom and Modern Tools**: Drawing from the insights of great thinkers and integrating contemporary practices like visualization and neuroscience, this book bridges ancient principles with modern relevance.

3. **Interactive Exercises and Templates**:
   Each chapter includes actionable exercises, journaling prompts, and habit-building strategies to ensure immediate application.
4. **Stories of Real-Life Transformation**:
   Through relatable examples, you'll see how individuals from diverse backgrounds used RightQs to overcome obstacles, achieve goals, and find fulfillment.
5. **Adaptability for All Audiences**:
   Whether you're a student, a professional, or someone seeking spiritual growth, this book offers universally applicable tools to align with your personal goals and aspirations.

This is not just a book to read—it is a companion to inspire action, encourage reflection, and foster meaningful change in your life.

How This Book Can Transform Your Life

Transformation begins with intention, and RightQs are the catalyst for that transformation. By embracing the principles in this book, you'll:

- **Break Free from Limiting Beliefs**: Challenge self-doubt and reframe negative thought patterns.
- **Cultivate Resilience**: Develop the mental and emotional strength to navigate life's challenges with grace.
- **Discover Clarity**: Identify your core values and align your actions with your aspirations.
- **Enhance Relationships**: Use RightQs to foster empathy, understanding, and meaningful connections.
- **Achieve Personal Growth**: Set and achieve goals that resonate with your true purpose.

This book doesn't just offer insights—it provides a practical roadmap to help you turn intention into action, enabling lasting growth and fulfillment.

Let these pages inspire you to reflect, realign, and thrive. The answers you seek are closer than you think; they begin with the right questions.

Unlocking the Path to Transformation

Transformation begins with a single step: asking the right question. At its core, this process aligns your thoughts, actions, and purpose with your natural essence. This book introduces **RightQs**, intentional prompts designed to unlock clarity, inspire growth, and create meaningful actions.

RightQs act as a compass, guiding you through life's complexities with confidence and focus. Whether you are seeking career direction, strengthening relationships, or enhancing your well-being, RightQs provide a simple yet profound framework for uncovering practical and fulfilling solutions.

The Power of Intention

As the Prophet Muhammad ﷺ (peace be upon him) said:

" إِنَّمَا الأَعْمَالُ بِالنِّيَّاتِ "

(Actions are judged by intentions.)

This timeless wisdom emphasizes that the value of any action begins with its intention. Sincere and purposeful intentions bring depth and meaning to your efforts, paving the way for lasting growth and fulfillment.

Whether your goals are personal, professional, or spiritual, grounding your intentions ensures that each step you take aligns with your values and aspirations.

Growth Beyond Boundaries

True transformation is not limited by geography, culture, or circumstances—it is a universal journey. While personal effort plays a vital role, **all growth ultimately stems from divine guidance and mercy**. Aligning your intentions with a higher purpose opens the door to meaningful change that reaches beyond individual limitations.

Progress is a journey of small, deliberate choices. RightQs serve as your guide, helping you navigate challenges while staying true to what matters most.

A Reminder for Life

"Watch your thoughts, for they become words. Watch your words, for they become actions. Watch your actions, for they become habits. Watch your habits, for they become character. Watch your character, for they become your destiny."

This wisdom reminds us that transformation begins with the smallest shifts—in thought, intention, and perspective. By nurturing intentional thoughts and mindful actions, you shape not only your decisions but the course of your life.

An Invitation to Growth

This book is your companion on a journey of reflection and self-discovery. As you explore its ideas and exercises, root your intentions in personal development and a deeper connection to your true essence. Through sincerity, clarity, and purposeful action, may you find the path to a fulfilling and meaningful life.

Abdullah Khan

About the Author

Abdullah Khan is a Digital Entrepreneur, visionary thinker, and the founder of *Words of Wisdom*, a platform dedicated to inspiring intentional living through meaningful content. His journey from humble beginnings to becoming a source of guidance for those seeking clarity and purpose reflects his deep understanding of the challenges and opportunities in today's world.

Blending timeless wisdom with actionable strategies, Abdullah empowers individuals to discover clarity, embrace purpose, and live with intention. His approach combines spiritual insights with modern tools, making his message relatable and impactful for readers from diverse backgrounds.

Through *The Right Question*, Abdullah invites you to embark on a transformative journey of self-discovery and growth. This book is just the beginning. With an unwavering commitment to making personal development accessible and meaningful, Abdullah looks forward to accompanying readers on more enriching journeys in his future works.

Learn more and join the community at:

www.wordsofwisdom.in

CHAPTER 1. THE POWER OF THE RIGHT QUESTION

Why Questions Shape Our Reality

The questions we ask shape the way we think, feel, and act. Every decision, every action, begins with a question—whether spoken aloud or lingering silently in our minds. Questions direct our focus, influence our emotions, and guide our responses to life's challenges.

Consider this: when faced with a setback, asking, "Why does this always happen to me?" keeps you trapped in frustration. However, shifting the question to, "What can I learn from this experience?" transforms the situation into an opportunity for growth. Questions are not just tools; they are the framework for how we build our reality.

Understanding the Natural Essence of Being Human

At the core of every individual lies the innate curiosity to understand and grow. This natural essence drives us to seek answers, discover purpose, and connect deeply with ourselves and others. However, modern life often disconnects us from this essence, replacing reflective inquiry with fleeting distractions.

By asking intentional, purposeful questions—what we call *RightQs*—we reconnect with this essence. RightQs guide us to align our thoughts and actions with our values, helping us uncover clarity, gratitude, and resilience in the process.

The Neuroscience Behind RightQs: How Questions Transform the Mind

Modern neuroscience reveals that asking questions activates the brain's Reticular Activating System (RAS), a network responsible for filtering information and determining what deserves attention. This system ensures that our brain focuses on what aligns with our current thoughts and goals, making questions a powerful tool for shaping reality.

Example: When you ask a constructive question, like "What small steps can I take to improve my well-being?" the RAS prioritizes information in your environment that supports your goal. For instance, you might notice a flyer for a yoga class or recall a conversation about healthy eating that had previously gone unnoticed. Conversely, negative questions, such as "Why does nothing ever go right for me?" reinforce patterns of doubt by filtering in evidence of obstacles rather than solutions.

Practical Insight: Think of your brain as a search engine. When you type in a specific query, like "best ways to stay healthy," it filters irrelevant information and highlights results that match your question Similarly, RightQs focus your brain on growth and possibility.

A study published in *Frontiers in Psychology* (2018) demonstrated that intentional questioning enhances neural activity in areas associated with problem-solving and learning. This activation strengthens the brain's ability to adapt and respond constructively to challenges. By framing empowering RightQs, you leverage this natural process to create actionable pathways for success and personal growth.

Everyday Transformations Through RightQs

1. **Career Clarity**: A young professional struggling with career choices asks, "What skills can I develop to pursue my passion?" This question leads to enrolling in a course that ultimately shapes their career path.
2. **Managing Responsibilities**: A parent overwhelmed with daily tasks reframes their self-critical question, "Why can't I manage everything?" into, "What small, manageable tasks can I prioritize today?" This shift reduces stress and increases productivity.
3. **Health and Well-Being**: Someone feeling physically unwell asks, "Why am I always tired?" Instead, they reframe it to, "What daily habit can I change to improve my energy levels?" leading to a healthier lifestyle.

Practical Examples

- **Mehtab's Story**:
  Mehtab, a teacher, felt disconnected from her profession. By asking herself, *"What difference can I make in one student's life today?"* she discovered renewed purpose. Small actions—like encouraging a struggling student or sharing a story of perseverance—not only transformed her day but reignited her passion for teaching.

- **Hamid's Story**:
  Hamid, a small business owner, struggled with financial setbacks. Instead of dwelling on *"Why do I keep facing these problems?"* he reframed his focus to, *"What steps can I take today to rebuild my finances?"*
  This question prompted him to seek professional advice and implement a new budgeting system. Over time, Hamid stabilized his business and felt empowered by his proactive approach.

These stories highlight the power of intentional questioning in transforming uncertainty into actionable growth.

How to Use RightQs Effectively

1. **Start Simple**:
   Begin with questions focusing on achievable actions.
   Example: *"What one thing can I do today to make progress?"*

2. **Stay Curious**:
   Approach challenges with wonder.
   Example: *"What opportunities might this situation present?"*

3. **Reflect Regularly**:
   Use journaling to track how RightQs shape your decisions and outcomes.

RightQs are more than a mental exercise—they are a way of life. As you integrate them into daily routines, you'll move from uncertainty to intentionality, uncovering a deeper connection to your true purpose.

Turning Questions into Actions: A Practical Flow

1. **Question**: *"What one positive step can I take?"*
2. **Thought**: *"I can start small and build from here."*
3. **Emotion**: *Hope replaces doubt.*
4. **Action**: *Implement the small step.*
5. **Outcome**: *Progress builds confidence.*

This flow demonstrates how the RightQs you ask can transform abstract thoughts into purposeful actions, ultimately creating meaningful results.

A Call to Reflection and Action

This book invites you to reflect on the questions you ask daily and how they shape your life. The answers you seek are not far; they are within reach, waiting for the right questions to bring them to light.

As you explore these pages, prepare to embrace a transformative journey—one guided by curiosity, purpose, and the profound power of asking the right questions.

Key Thought:
"The questions we ask determine the paths we walk."

CHAPTER 2: THE ART OF INTENTIONAL QUESTIONING

Why Questions Matter

The questions we ask shape the way we perceive and interact with the world. Every major breakthrough or change starts with a single question, one that sparks curiosity, self-reflection, and action. Yet, not all questions lead to clarity and growth—some can reinforce doubt, fear, and stagnation.

For example, asking, "Why can't I ever succeed?" invites feelings of inadequacy and hopelessness. On the other hand, reframing the inquiry to, "What steps can I take today to achieve my goals?" opens the door to solutions and forward momentum. RightQs are designed to do exactly that—shift your focus, reframe your perspective, and guide you toward clarity and purpose.

Questions as Catalysts for Change

Imagine standing at a crossroads, uncertain of which path to take. The questions you ask in that moment have the power to shape your future. Thoughtfully crafted questions can act as a bridge between uncertainty and clarity. Instead of passively enduring setbacks, the right questions can lead us toward empowered action and personal growth.

Transformative RightQs:

- "Why am I capable of finding a solution to this problem?"
- "Why am I confident in my ability to achieve my goals?"
- "What blessings am I surrounded by that bring joy to my life?"

Every question has the potential to shift your focus, influence your emotions, and inspire action. Intentional questioning becomes a guiding compass, turning challenges into opportunities for growth.

Real-Life Inspired Stories: Transformations in Action

1. **Sarah's Story (Health)**: Struggling with chronic fatigue, Sarah constantly asked herself, "Why can't I feel better?" This left her trapped in frustration. By reframing her question to, "What one small change can I make today to improve

my energy levels?" Sarah began walking for ten minutes daily. Over time, this simple habit evolved into a full wellness routine, restoring her vitality and confidence.

2. **Amir's Story (Spirituality)**: Feeling disconnected from his purpose, Amir asked, "What can I do to feel more grateful?" This question led him to start a daily gratitude journal, transforming his perspective and deepening his sense of contentment.

3. **Lila's Story (Career)**: Unsure about her professional future, Lila frequently asked, "What's the point of all this effort?" After learning about RightQs, she reframed her question to, "How can I align my work with my passions?" This inspired her to pursue a certification program, which eventually led to a fulfilling career pivot.

Practical Exercises to Integrate RightQs into Your Life

Morning Inquiry: Begin each day with an intentional RightQ that sets a positive tone.

Example: "What can I do today to align my actions with my values?"

Reflection Time: Identify recurring negative questions in your thoughts. Reframe each into a RightQ.

Example:

- Negative: "Why do things always go wrong?"
- RightQ: "What lesson can I learn from this setback?"

Evening Journaling Prompt: Conclude your day by reflecting on a meaningful RightQ.

- Example: "What am I grateful for today, and how can I carry this gratitude into tomorrow?"

Themes for Deeper Focus

Health: RightQs for physical well-being:

- "What one habit can I adopt today to feel healthier?"
- "How can I create more balance between rest and activity?"

Spirituality: Subtle RightQs for inner growth:

- "How can I show gratitude for the blessings in my life?"
- "What small action can I take to bring more peace into my day?"

Relationships: Questions to deepen connections:

- "How can I show appreciation to someone I value today?"
- "What can I do to improve communication with those I care about?"

Crafting Transformative RightQs

Not all questions have the power to inspire change. A RightQ is intentionally crafted to empower and guide you. It is:

- **Positive in Framing**: Avoids negativity and invites constructive reflection.
    - Weak: "Why am I such a failure?"
    - RightQ: "What have I learned from my past experiences that I can use now?"
- **Actionable in Focus**: Encourages taking small, purposeful steps.
    - Weak: "When will I ever succeed?"
    - RightQ: "What is one thing I can do today to move closer to my goal?"
- **Value-Oriented**: Aligns with your personal beliefs and aspirations.
    - Weak: "Why don't I have what they have?"
    - RightQ: "What unique strengths can I cultivate to achieve my own vision?"

Shifting from Passive to Active Thinking

The transition from passive to active thinking is at the heart of intentional questioning. Passive thoughts often revolve around why situations feel out of our control: *"Why does this always happen to me?"* Active thinking, fueled by RightQs, shifts focus to possibilities: **"What can I do to influence this outcome?"**

Closing Thought

The art of intentional questioning empowers us to navigate life's uncertainties with clarity and courage. By aligning your questions with your values and aspirations, you unlock a path of growth, purpose, and resilience.

"Empowered questions lead to empowered lives."

CHAPTER 3: CLARITY THROUGH REFLECTION

Key Insight

Reflection is the bridge between experience and wisdom. It transforms fleeting moments into lasting lessons, helping us discover clarity, strength, and purpose in a noisy world.

Discovering Your True Self

Self-discovery is the cornerstone of meaningful growth. Understanding your true self requires reflection—an intentional pause to connect with your values, strengths, and aspirations. Without this process, we risk navigating life on autopilot, reacting to external demands rather than aligning with our inner purpose.

Consider this: How often do you reflect on who you are beyond your roles and responsibilities? Reflection creates a mirror to see beyond the surface, uncovering your core essence and unique potential.

RightQs are essential tools in this process. They guide your reflection, turning abstract thoughts into meaningful insights. When you ask, "What truly matters to me?" or "What can I do today to honor my values?" you create a pathway toward self-awareness and purposeful living.

The Role of Reflection in Personal Growth

Reflection is not merely looking back; it is the art of extracting lessons and insights from our experiences to shape our future. By consistently engaging in reflection, we build emotional intelligence, resilience, and clarity. Reflection is the compass that points us toward intentional growth.

1. **Emotional Growth**: Regular reflection helps identify patterns in our emotions, guiding us to manage them more effectively.
2. **Cognitive Growth**: Reflection sharpens our decision-making by connecting past experiences with future possibilities.
3. **Spiritual Growth**: Reflecting on our blessings fosters gratitude, deepening our connection to the world around us.

Guided RightQs for Introspection

To harness the power of reflection, ask intentional questions that guide you inward. These RightQs are designed to uncover insights, align your thoughts with your values, and inspire purposeful actions:

1. **General Introspection**:
    - "What are my core values, and how do they shape my decisions?"
    - "What past experiences have taught me the most about myself?"
2. **Navigating Challenges**:
    - "What can I learn from this setback?"
    - "What resources or strengths can I use to overcome this obstacle?"
3. **Future Planning**:
    - "What steps can I take today to move closer to my aspirations?"
    - "How can I align my actions with the person I strive to become?"
4. **Exploring Strengths and Values**:
    - "What am I proud of accomplishing recently?"

- "What values guide my decisions?"

5. **Processing Emotions**:
    - "What emotion am I experiencing right now, and why?"
    - "What action can I take to address this feeling?"
6. **Setting Intentions**:
    - "What do I want to focus on this week?"
    - "What small step can I take today toward my goals?"

Practical Exercises for Reflection

1. **Morning Reflection**:
   - Begin your day by asking, "What is one intentional action I can take today to align with my values?"
2. **Midday Pause**:
   - Take a five-minute break during the day to ask, "What is working well so far, and what can I adjust to improve my focus?"
3. **Mirror Reflection**:
   - Look in the mirror and ask yourself, "Am I living in alignment with my values today?"
4. **Reflection Walks**:
   - Take a walk in nature and reflect on a single RightQ, such as, "What brings me peace and fulfillment?"
5. **Evening Journaling**:
   - Conclude your day by writing about, "What did I learn today about myself or others?"

Themes for Deeper Reflection

Self-Awareness:

- "What habits or behaviors no longer serve me?"
- "How can I nurture my unique strengths?"

Gratitude:

- "What am I grateful for today?"
- "How can I express appreciation to someone who has impacted my life?"

Personal Growth:

- "What fear can I face to unlock my potential?"
- "What small step can I take today toward self-improvement?"

Health:

- "What habit can I adopt to feel more energetic?"
- "How can I nurture my well-being today?"

Relationships:

- "How can I show appreciation to someone I care about?"
- "What can I do to deepen my connection with a loved one?"

Purpose:

- "What gives my life meaning?"
- "How can I align my daily actions with my long-term goals?"

Lessons from Great Thinkers

Reflection has been the cornerstone of wisdom across centuries. Thinkers like Socrates emphasized the unexamined life, while spiritual leaders like Imam Ghazali called for introspection to align the heart and mind. Their teachings remind us that reflection is a universal path to enlightenment.

Quotes to Inspire Your Reflection Practice

1. "Knowing yourself is the beginning of all wisdom." —Aristotle
2. "Man has been given a tongue and two ears that he may listen more than speak." —Hazrat Ali ؓ
3. "Reflection is the lamp that lights the path to clarity." —Anonymous
4. "What lies behind us and what lies before us are tiny matters compared to what lies within us." —Ralph Waldo Emerson

---

Key Takeaways

- Reflection deepens self-awareness by uncovering values and aspirations.
- It fosters emotional intelligence, resilience, and intentional growth.
- Guided RightQs are practical tools for aligning thoughts and actions with your true self.

Closing Thought

Reflection is a bridge to self-discovery. By embracing the power of intentional questioning, you unlock the clarity needed to navigate life's complexities. Start today with a single question: "What can I learn from this moment?"

"Through reflection, we transform experiences into wisdom."

CHAPTER 4: OVERCOMING BARRIERS

Key Insight

Barriers like resistance and self-doubt are not walls but doors waiting to be opened. With the right questions, we can transform these obstacles into pathways for growth. Every barrier is an opportunity in disguise, waiting for the right question to uncover its potential.

RightQs empower us to shift our mindset and uncover the growth potential hidden within challenges. By starting with one intentional question, we can unlock doors to confidence, clarity, and action.

Identifying Resistance and Self-Doubt

Resistance and self-doubt often act as invisible barriers, preventing us from reaching our full potential. These barriers manifest as inner voices whispering, "You're not good enough," or "This isn't worth the effort." Left unchecked, these thoughts can paralyze progress, keeping us stuck in cycles of fear and procrastination.

Mawlānā Rūmī said: "Try not to resist the changes that come your way. Instead, let life live through you."

RightQs help us face these barriers, reframing them as opportunities for growth and self-discovery.

Transforming Resistance with RightQs

Resistance often stems from fear—fear of failure, fear of change, or fear of the unknown. RightQs are a powerful tool for confronting and overcoming resistance. They challenge limiting beliefs and create space for solutions by shifting focus from problems to possibilities.

Examples of RightQs to Overcome Resistance:

- "What can I learn from this challenge?"
- "What is one small step I can take to move forward?"
- "How can I reframe this obstacle as an opportunity?"

By repeatedly asking empowering questions, you train your mind to focus on solutions and growth, gradually weakening the grip of resistance.

Breaking the Cycle of Self-Doubt

Self-doubt thrives on negative thought patterns and past failures. RightQs encourage introspection and foster confidence by focusing on past achievements and potential.

Examples of RightQs to Address Self-Doubt:

- "What evidence do I have of my past successes?"
- "How have I demonstrated resilience in similar situations before?"
- "What unique strengths can I bring to this challenge?"

Practical Exercise: Write down three recurring doubts or fears. For each, craft a RightQ that reframes it into an empowering perspective. Reflect on these RightQs daily to internalize positive thinking.

Overcoming Procrastination with RightQs

Procrastination often stems from overwhelm or fear of imperfection. Using RightQs can help break tasks into manageable steps and reignite motivation.

Examples of RightQs to Overcome Procrastination:

- "What is one small, actionable step I can take right now?"
- "How will completing this task bring me closer to my goals?"

Practical Exercise:

1. Identify a task you've been avoiding.
2. Ask: "What is one thing I can do to start this task today?"
3. Write down your progress each evening to build momentum and accountability.

Lessons from Real-Life Transformations

Case Study 1: Overcoming Procrastination

- **Challenge**: Faheem, a college student, constantly procrastinated on assignments, believing he lacked discipline.
- **RightQ Applied**: "What small step can I take right now to start?"
- **Outcome**: By breaking tasks into manageable steps, Faheem gradually built momentum, boosting his productivity and confidence.

Case Study 2: Facing Fear of Failure

- **Challenge**: Shehnaz wanted to launch her own business but feared it might fail.
- **RightQ Applied**: "What resources and skills can I leverage to minimize risks?"
- **Outcome**: Shehnaz sought mentorship, created a detailed plan, and successfully launched her business, transforming fear into motivation.

Case Study 3: Rediscovering Passion in Work

- **Challenge**: Mehtab, a teacher, felt disconnected from her profession and doubted her impact.

- **RightQ Applied**: "What one action can I take today to inspire my students?"
- **Outcome**: Mehtab introduced creative projects in her classroom, reigniting her passion for teaching and strengthening her connection with students.

The Role of Self-Compassion in Overcoming Barriers

One of the most effective tools for overcoming resistance and doubt is self-compassion. Recognizing and accepting your struggles without judgment creates space for growth. Mawlānā Rūmī reminds us: **"Be like a tree and let the dead leaves drop."**

Self-compassion helps us let go of past failures and embrace the possibilities of new beginnings.

Practical Application:

- Reflect on a recent mistake or failure and ask yourself: "What can I learn from this without criticizing myself?"
- Pair this reflection with a self-compassion practice, such as writing a kind letter to yourself acknowledging your efforts and strengths.

RightQs for Self-Compassion:

- "What can I do today to treat myself with kindness?"
- "How can I learn from this mistake without self-criticism?"
- "What strengths have I shown in facing challenges before?"

Practical Exercises for Transformation

Daily RightQs:

Begin each day by asking: "What is one small win I can achieve today to build my confidence?"

Visualization for Resistance:

Close your eyes and visualize overcoming a specific challenge. For example, if you're preparing for a presentation, imagine yourself confidently delivering it. Pair this visualization with the question: "What preparation can I do today to feel more ready?"

Reflection Prompts

Take a moment to consider:

- "What recurring doubts or fears hold me back?"
- "What empowering questions can I ask to overcome them?"
- "What strengths can I build on to face future challenges?"

Write your responses and revisit them regularly to track your progress.

Key Takeaways for Overcoming Barriers

- Resistance and self-doubt are natural but can be transformed through intentional questioning.
- RightQs empower you to focus on solutions, not problems.
- Self-compassion is essential for breaking free from limiting beliefs and fostering growth.
- Daily practices like journaling and visualization reinforce positive change.

Closing Thought

Overcoming barriers isn't about erasing fear or doubt—it's about transforming them into stepping stones for growth. With the power of RightQs and self-compassion, you can dismantle limiting beliefs and unlock your potential.

"When doubt whispers, let your questions roar with purpose."

CHAPTER 5: BUILDING CONFIDENCE AND RESILIENCE

Key Insight

Confidence is the belief in your ability to succeed; resilience is the determination to persevere when challenges arise. Imagine standing at the edge of a daunting task—your next step can either be paralyzed by fear or propelled by purpose. With the right mindset and questions, this moment becomes a chance to thrive. Together, they form the foundation for navigating life's complexities. With RightQs, you can cultivate both, transforming self-doubt into self-assurance and challenges into opportunities for growth.

The Power of Positive Reframing

Life's challenges can either break us or build us, depending on how we perceive them. Positive reframing helps shift the focus from failure to opportunity, allowing us to see setbacks as stepping stones. For example, when a project falls short of expectations, asking 'What did I learn from this experience?' can reveal valuable insights, turning the setback into a growth opportunity.

Examples of Positive Reframing RightQs:

- "What lesson can I take from this experience to grow stronger?"
- "How does this challenge align with my long-term goals?"
- "What small success can I celebrate today?"

Strengthening Inner Belief Systems

A resilient belief system is built by consistently focusing on strengths, past achievements, and the ability to adapt. RightQs serve as a foundation to nurture confidence by redirecting attention to personal growth and self-worth.

Examples of RightQs to Strengthen Inner Belief Systems:

- "What past achievements prove my ability to succeed?"
- "How can I adapt and overcome in this situation?"
- "What values drive me to persevere?"

Real-Life Inspired Stories: Transformations in Action

Case Study 1: Building Confidence through Public Speaking

- **Challenge**: Arshad, a software engineer, struggled with speaking in team meetings due to fear of judgment.
- **RightQ Applied**: "What preparation can I do to feel more confident?"
- **Outcome**: By rehearsing key points and seeking feedback, Arshad gradually gained confidence, eventually leading discussions with ease.

Case Study 2: Cultivating Resilience After Career Loss

- **Challenge**: Laura, a marketing professional, was laid off and doubted her abilities.
- **RightQ Applied**: "What skills can I develop to rebuild my career?"
- **Outcome**: Laura enrolled in a digital marketing certification, networked actively, and secured a fulfilling role that aligned with her passions.

Case Study 3: Caregiver Rebuilding Balance

- **Challenge**: Farida, a full-time caregiver, felt overwhelmed and burnt out.
- **RightQ Applied**: "What small act of self-care can I practice today?"
- **Outcome**: Farida introduced 15 minutes of daily mindfulness exercises, which rejuvenated her energy, reduced her stress levels by 30% over a month, and improved her ability to care for others more effectively.

Practical Exercises to Build Confidence and Resilience

- Write down three of your biggest accomplishments.
- Reflect on the questions: "What strengths helped me achieve these?" and "How can I apply these strengths today?"

Daily Confidence Booster:

- Begin each day with the RightQ: "What one action today will strengthen my confidence?"
- Reflect on small wins at the end of the day.

Resilience Journaling:

- Write about a past challenge you overcame. Pair this reflection with: "What qualities helped me succeed, and how can I use them again?"

Visualization Practice:

- Close your eyes and visualize successfully overcoming a current challenge. For example, if you're preparing for a presentation or job interview, imagine yourself speaking clearly, confidently engaging your audience, and responding thoughtfully. Pair this with the RightQ: 'What steps can I take today to feel fully prepared for this moment?'

Reflection Prompts

Take a moment to consider:

- "What fears or doubts are limiting my confidence?"
- "What RightQs can I ask to shift my focus to solutions and strengths?"
- "What past challenges have shaped my resilience?"
- "What values drive my confidence in uncertain times?"

Key Takeaways for Building Confidence and Resilience

- Positive reframing transforms setbacks into opportunities for growth.
- RightQs strengthen belief systems by highlighting strengths and values.
- Confidence and resilience grow through daily practice and intentional reflection.
- Visualization and journaling enhance self-awareness and action.

Interactive Exercises

Daily Tracker for Confidence and Resilience:

Create a simple table to track daily wins, challenges faced, and the RightQs used to navigate them.

Example:

Date	Win of the Day	Challenge Overcome	RightQ Used
[Date]	Completed a key task	Overcame hesitation in a call	"What one step can I take now?"

RightQ Practice Template:

- Reflect on recurring doubts and reframe them using RightQs.
- Example:
  - **Doubt**: "I'm not good at this."
  - **RightQ**: "What can I learn to improve?"

Closing Thought

Confidence and resilience are not about avoiding challenges but embracing them as opportunities to grow. Take your first step today by asking a RightQ that shifts your focus from fear to possibility. What will you do now to move forward with confidence? With RightQs, you hold the power to rewrite the narrative of self-doubt and step into your full potential.

"Confidence is not about being fearless but about facing fear with purpose."

CHAPTER 6: CULTIVATING GRATITUDE AND CONTENTMENT

Gratitude transforms the way we perceive our lives. It shifts focus from what we lack to what we have, fostering contentment and joy.

The Holy Qur'an highlights the transformative power of gratitude in **"If you are grateful, I will certainly give you more."** (14:7)
This verse is a divine promise that expressing gratitude leads to an increase in blessings. Gratitude is not just a virtue but a powerful tool for personal growth. It fosters an optimistic mindset, improves emotional well-being, and creates opportunities for further achievements. By cherishing what we have, we open the door to contentment, fostering peace and growth in our lives.

Mawlānā Rūmīؒ beautifully said: ***"Wear gratitude like a cloak, and it will feed every corner of your life."***

When we focus on gratitude, we create a foundation for spiritual and emotional growth, allowing us to shift from challenges to possibilities.

The Power of Gratitude in Shaping Perspective

Gratitude shifts our focus from what we lack to what we have. It is a deliberate practice that nurtures thankfulness and opens the way to contentment—both spiritually and emotionally.

For example, when overwhelmed by stress, asking *"What am I grateful for in this moment?"* can instantly redirect focus to a supportive friend or a recent accomplishment. Gratitude aligns us with inner peace and clarity, helping us navigate life's complexities.

Gratitude as a Path to Fulfillment

Gratitude is not just an emotion; it is a deliberate practice that shapes how we perceive and interact with the world. By focusing on blessings, big or small, gratitude creates a ripple effect of positivity in our lives. It nurtures emotional resilience, reduces stress, and deepens our connections with others.

Gratitude also acts as a mirror, reflecting the beauty of life's moments that we often take for granted. For example, appreciating the simple joy of a heartfelt conversation or the warmth of sunlight can shift your perspective, leading to a more fulfilling life.

Reflective Questions for Gratitude:

- "What small blessings have brought me joy today?"
- "Who in my life deserves my appreciation, and how can I express it?"

Insights from The Alchemy of Happiness

Imam Ghazaliۃ, in *The Alchemy of Happiness*, emphasizes that true happiness lies in acknowledging the Creator's blessings and using them responsibly. Reflective questions inspired by his teachings include:

- "How can I honor the blessings I've been given today?"
- "What actions reflect gratitude for the opportunities I've received?"
- "How can I use my gratitude to deepen my connection with others and my Creator?"

Practical Exercise Inspired by Imam Ghazaliۃ: Reflect on a recent success and ask: "How can I use this success to benefit others as an act of gratitude?"

Commit to one meaningful action within the week to make a positive impact.

Shifting from Scarcity to Contentment

Many of us focus on what we lack, creating a mindset of scarcity that limits our potential. Shifting to contentment involves appreciating what we already have and recognizing the resources and strengths within us.

For instance, instead of thinking, *"I never have enough time,"* reframing the thought to, *"What priorities can I focus on today to maximize my time?"* opens the door to productive solutions. This shift not only eases frustration but also fosters creativity and hope.

Practical Exercise:

1. Write down three areas where you feel scarcity (e.g., time, finances, relationships).
2. Reframe each thought with a question that emphasizes contentment.
   Example:
   Scarcity: *"I don't have enough money to enjoy life."*

Contentment Question: *"What simple joys can I experience today that don't require spending?"*

This shift helps us see challenges as opportunities and align our actions with a mindset of gratitude.

The Neuroscience of Gratitude

Modern neuroscience reveals that practicing gratitude rewires the brain, increasing dopamine and serotonin levels—chemicals responsible for happiness. A study published in *Frontiers in Psychology* (2018) highlights that regular gratitude practices enhance neural sensitivity in reward-related brain regions, promoting long-term emotional well-being. Similarly, research by Harvard Medical School found that gratitude can make individuals 25% happier. By focusing on gratitude, we train our minds to notice positivity, fostering resilience and peace.

Practical Gratitude Exercises

Gratitude Journaling:

Every evening, write three things you are grateful for and pair each with a reflective question. Example:
Gratitude: "I'm thankful for my supportive friends."
Question: "How can I show my appreciation to them tomorrow?"

Morning Gratitude Reflections:

Start your day by asking: "What am I looking forward to today, and how can I make the most of it?"

Contentment Visualization:

Close your eyes and visualize fulfilling relationships, meaningful work, or personal well-being. Pair this with: "What steps can I take today to align my actions with this vision?"

Exercises for Diverse Backgrounds:

For Students: Reflect on a teacher's guidance and ask, "How can I show gratitude for the support I've received in my studies?"

For Caregivers: Reflect on moments of connection with loved ones and ask, "What small act of kindness can I do today to express my care?"

For Professionals: Reflect on a recent achievement at work and ask, "How can I use this success to mentor or assist a colleague?"

Real-Life Inspired Stories: Transformations in Action

Case Study 1: Embracing Gratitude After Loss

- **Challenge**: David, a small business owner, faced the loss of his family's generational business during an economic downturn. Struggling with grief, he found it hard to see the good in life.
- **Reflection Applied**: "What blessings remain, and how can I honor them?"
- **Outcome**: Through daily gratitude journaling, David rediscovered his purpose, started a new venture creating handmade furniture, and gained financial stability while earning community appreciation.

Case Study 2: Shifting from Scarcity to Contentment

- **Challenge**: Nia, a freelance writer, felt she lacked resources to grow her client base and worried about financial instability.
- **Reflection Applied**: "What skills and connections do I already have to take the next step?"
- **Outcome**: Nia collaborated with a fellow writer, secured a lucrative project, and developed an online portfolio that attracted new clients, boosting her confidence and career stability.

Case Study 3: Creating Value Through Talents

- **Challenge**: Akash, a graphic designer, doubted whether his talents could make a meaningful impact.
- **Reflection Applied**: "How can I use my talents to create value for others?"
- **Outcome**: Akash volunteered his design skills to a nonprofit, gained recognition, and expanded his professional network, transforming self-doubt into confidence.

Reflection Prompts

- "What blessings in my life am I currently overlooking?"
- "How can I shift my focus from scarcity to contentment today?"
- "What actions can I take to express gratitude meaningfully?"
- "What strengths have helped me overcome difficulties in the past?"
- "What daily habits can help me sustain a mindset of gratitude?"

Key Takeaways for Cultivating Gratitude and Contentment

- Gratitude rewires the brain for positivity and enhances overall well-being.
- Reflective questions pivot thinking from scarcity to contentment, creating opportunities for growth.
- Daily practices like journaling and visualization reduce stress, foster positivity, and clarify goals.

- Shifting focus to blessings reveals hidden opportunities in challenges.

Call to Action

Take a moment to reflect on the blessings in your life. Write down one small action you can take today to express gratitude meaningfully. Share your reflections or experiences with gratitude to inspire others and create a ripple effect of positivity.

Closing Thought

Gratitude and contentment are choices we make every day. By reflecting intentionally, we align our thoughts with positivity and possibility, transforming our reality into one of fulfillment and peace.

"Gratitude turns what we have into enough and opens the door to more."

CHAPTER 6: QUESTIONS FOR PURPOSE AND FULFILMENT

Understanding the Purpose of Life

Every human being yearns to find meaning—a purpose that illuminates their path and brings clarity to their actions. The Holy Qur'an beautifully anchors this pursuit in several verses, urging reflection and intentional living.

"And why should I not worship the One who created me and to whom you will be returned?" (Surah Ya-Sin 36:22)

This verse reminds us that life is not random but deeply rooted in meaning and our connection to the Creator. It calls us to reflect on the purpose of our existence and align our actions with higher values.

Surah At-Tur 52:35 challenges us to contemplate: **"Were they created by nothing, or were they the creators?"**

This question invites us to recognize the intricate design of creation and the signs of divine wisdom within and around us.

Surah An-Nisa 4:39 highlights the practical aspect of living purposefully:

"And what burden Were it on them if they had faith in Allah and in the Last Day, and they spent out of what Allah hath given them for sustenance?"

Here, the verse reminds us that fulfilling our purpose is not a burden but a pathway to ease and spiritual fulfilment, urging us to give back and contribute positively to our surroundings.

In Surah Adh-Dhariyat 51:56, Allah (Glorified & Exalted), states:

"And I did not create the jinn and mankind except to worship Me."

Imam Ja'far Sadiqؑ: Guiding Minds Toward Truth and Purpose

Imam Ja'far Sadiqؑ, renowned for his wisdom, eloquently refuted atheism in his famous debate with an atheist. He demonstrated through reasoning that the harmony of creation points unmistakably to a Creator. Using the analogy of a ship, he explained: *"If a ship, left without a navigator, would inevitably drift aimlessly, how then could the universe, infinitely more complex, exist without purpose?"*

The atheist was left speechless as Imam Ja'far Sadiqؑ dismantled the notion of purposelessness by highlighting:

- The intricate order in nature: *"Who orchestrates the rising and setting of the sun, the flow of rivers, and the cycles of life?"*
- The innate yearning for meaning in every human being: *"If the universe was without purpose, why do we seek fulfillment and alignment in our lives?"*
- The impossibility of self-creation: **"Were you created by nothing, or did you create yourself?"** (Surah At-Tur 52:35)

Reflective Questions from the Debate:

- "Who is the navigator behind the harmony I witness in the universe?"
- "What signs of purpose and design do I see within myself and the world around me?"
- "If the universe points to a Creator, how can I align my life with that truth?"

This profound debate not only silenced the atheist but also inspired generations to reflect deeply on their purpose and existence.

Discovering and Aligning with Purpose

Purpose is not something we must create but something we uncover by reflecting on our innate strengths, passions, and values. By asking meaningful questions, we can align our daily actions with a higher purpose.

Reflective Questions for Discovering Purpose:

- "What activities make me feel truly alive?"
- "What impact do I want to leave in the lives of others?"
- "How can I align my daily actions with my core values?"

Practical Exercise:

1. Write down three moments when you felt deeply fulfilled.
2. Identify common themes or values present in those experiences.
3. Ask: *"How can I incorporate these values into my daily life?"*

Overcoming Obstacles to Fulfillment

The journey to fulfilling one's purpose is often fraught with challenges, including fear, doubt, and societal pressures. Imam Ja'far Sadiq taught that understanding one's inner strengths and divine purpose helps overcome these obstacles, turning trials into opportunities for growth.

For example, Surah An-Nisa 4:39 inspires us to act with faith and generosity, emphasizing that these actions lighten the journey rather than burden it.

Practical Exercise for Overcoming Obstacles:

1. Identify a recurring challenge or fear.
2. Write down a RightQ to reframe it positively. Example:
    - Fear: *"What if I fail?"*
    - RightQ: ***"What strengths have I used in the past to overcome similar challenges?"***

Creating a Life of Meaning

A meaningful life is built on intentional actions that reflect our higher purpose. It is not about grand achievements but about consistently aligning our daily choices with values that matter to us. This deliberate alignment transforms ordinary moments into opportunities for growth and fulfillment.

Surah Ya-Sin 36:22 reminds us of our ultimate return to the Creator, prompting us to live each day with intention. Asking, ***"What can I do today to bring myself closer to eternal success?"*** can guide our choices toward actions that create lasting impact.

Practical Examples of RightQs for Meaningful Living:

- "How can I use my skills to serve others today?"
- "What small act of kindness can I practice to make a difference?"
- "What legacy do I want to leave for future generations?"

Case Study:
Revitalizing Purpose Through Education

- **Challenge**: Zainab, a struggling single mother, felt overwhelmed by financial and personal challenges, believing her dreams of higher education were unattainable.
- **RightQ Applied**: "What small step can I take today to invest in my growth and inspire my children?"
- **Outcome**: Zainab began taking online courses, completing assignments during her children's nap times. Her efforts not only advanced her skills but also set an inspiring example for her children, proving that perseverance and purpose can create a ripple effect of positive change. Zainab's journey eventually inspired her to mentor other single mothers, creating a community of mutual support and empowerment.

Case Study:
Rediscovering Purpose in Retirement

- **Challenge**: Dastageer, a retired teacher, felt disconnected and unsure of how to spend his time meaningfully after years of service.
- **RightQ Applied**: "How can I use my knowledge to benefit others in my community?"
- **Outcome**: Dastageer began tutoring underprivileged students at a local community center, finding renewed purpose and joy in mentoring the next generation. His dedication not only helped students achieve academic milestones but also reignited his own sense of joy and fulfillment.

Reflection Prompts for Purpose Discovery

1. "What experiences have shaped who I am today?"
2. "What drives me to make a difference in my surroundings?"
3. "How can I align my talents with causes that matter to me?"

4. "What brings me peace and fulfillment in my daily life?"
5. "How can I turn a setback into a stepping stone toward purpose?"

Closing Thought

Discovering and living your purpose is a journey of reflection, intention, and action. As you align your actions with the Creator's guidance and the wisdom inherent in His creation, your life transforms into one of fulfillment and meaning. Each step you take toward your purpose strengthens your connection to Allah (Glorified & Exalted) and His creation, bringing clarity, peace, and eternal reward.

"The best among you are those who bring the greatest benefit to others." (Sunan al-Kubra)

CHAPTER 8: TURNING INSIGHTS INTO ACTION

The Transformative Power of intentional questioning

Understanding the power of intentional questioning is only the beginning. Real transformation occurs when we integrate these questions into our daily lives. For instance, Alex, a busy entrepreneur, began using the RightQ, ***"What is one impactful step I can take today?"*** This simple habit helped him prioritize his goals, delegate tasks effectively, and create a healthier work-life balance, showcasing the power of intentional questioning. This chapter provides practical tools and strategies to ensure intentional questioning becomes a natural part of your mindset, leading to clarity, growth, and purpose.

Mawlānā Rūmī◌ؒ beautifully said:
"As you start to walk on the way, the way appears."

With the right tools, you can navigate life's challenges and opportunities with confidence and intention.

The Power of Consistency

Consistency is the cornerstone of meaningful transformation. Just as repeated actions form habits, regularly practicing RightQs strengthens the mind's ability to focus on growth and clarity. Over time, these small, consistent efforts compound, creating lasting change in thought patterns and decision-making. Regularly practicing RightQs strengthens neural pathways, reinforcing positive thought patterns and empowering decision-making.

Practical Tips for Building Consistency:

1. **Start Small**: Begin with one RightQ each morning, such as:
   "What is one meaningful thing I can do today?"

2. **Set Reminders**: Use alarms, sticky notes, or digital tools to prompt reflection throughout the day.

3. **Track Progress**: Maintain a journal to document your RightQs and the insights they inspire. For instance, divide your journal into three sections: Morning Reflection, Midday Check-In, and Evening Reflection. A sample entry might include:

- **Morning RightQ**: **"What meaningful step can I take today?"**
- **Action Plan**: "I will schedule uninterrupted time for deep work."
- **Evening Reflection**: **"What did I learn today?** I learned that starting small tasks reduces my procrastination." Reflect weekly to identify patterns and growth.

Tools for Daily Integration

The Morning Mindset Practice:

Dedicate five minutes each morning to ask a RightQ that sets the tone for your day. Example: *"How can I align my actions with my values today?"*

Reflect on your response and write it down to solidify your intention.

For instance, Mehtab, a teacher, started her mornings with the question, *"How can I make today meaningful for my students?"* This simple practice helped her prioritize her goals, stay focused, and create impactful lessons, ultimately bringing more clarity and purpose to her day.

The RightQ Journal:

Create a dedicated space to document your questions, reflections, and progress.

Use prompts such as:

- *"What did I learn about myself today?"*
- *"What opportunities for growth did I notice?"*

Mindful Pauses:

Incorporate brief moments throughout your day to ask reflective questions.

Example:

- *"Am I focusing on what truly matters?"*
- *"How can I handle this situation with wisdom and grace?"*

Evening Reflection:

Conclude your day with gratitude and growth-focused RightQs.

Example:

- *"What am I thankful for today?"*
- *"What did I do well, and what can I improve tomorrow?"*

Quotes for Inspiration

- *"Small consistent actions lead to big transformations."*
- *"RightQs are the bridge between intention and action."*
- *"The questions you ask daily determine the life you create."*
- *"Your daily reflections shape the foundation of your future, turning thoughtful questions into a roadmap for achieving long-term goals and success."*

By turning insights into action, you create a life guided by purpose, clarity, and resilience. *"The life you build is shaped by the questions you consistently ask."* These tools are stepping stones to deeper practices, preparing you for sustained growth and fulfillment.

CHAPTER 9: TRANSFORMING TRIALS INTO TRIUMPHS

Turning Adversity into Growth

Life's challenges are not obstacles but chances to grow. Consider Shehnaz, a determined entrepreneur whose startup faced unexpected financial difficulties. Rather than giving in to despair, she asked herself, *"What strategies can I implement to sustain my business?"* This reflective question led her to innovate and ultimately expand her customer base.

Mawlānā Rūmī reminds us:
"Don't grieve. Anything you lose comes round in another form."

This chapter explores how reflection and resilience, guided by RightQs, can turn adversity into meaningful transformation and renewed purpose.

The Transformative Power of Reflection

Reflection allows us to pause, process, and derive meaning from difficult experiences. It provides mental clarity by helping us disentangle complex emotions and focus on actionable steps, while also fostering emotional stability by offering a space to acknowledge and navigate feelings constructively. It shifts our focus from immediate setbacks to long-term growth, transforming obstacles into valuable lessons.

Key RightQs for Reflection:

- *"What resources or strengths can I rely on to navigate this difficulty?"*
- *"What small step can I take today to regain clarity and direction?"*

Practical Exercise:

- After encountering a setback, dedicate 10 minutes to reflect and answer these RightQs in a journal.
- Revisit your responses periodically to track your growth and uncover patterns of resilience.

Stories of Resilience and Growth

1: Ateeq - Finding Opportunity in Career Setback

- **Challenge**: Ateeq, a mid-career professional, faced an unexpected layoff during a company restructure, leaving him anxious and questioning his abilities.
- **RightQ Applied**: *"What new skills can I develop to align with emerging opportunities?"*
- **Outcome**: Ateeq reflected on his strengths and pursued online certifications in data analytics, a high-demand field. He also sought mentorship from industry peers, which boosted his confidence and provided valuable insights. Within six months, he transitioned into a new role, leveraging his updated skills and rebuilding his confidence.

2: Noor - Turning Grief into Community Impact

- **Challenge**: Noor, a passionate educator, felt overwhelmed with grief and a deep sense of loss after losing her closest friend.
- **RightQ Applied**: *"How can I honor their legacy while finding healing?"*

- **Outcome**: Noor channeled her grief into action by establishing a community reading program in her friend's memory. This initiative not only promoted literacy but also provided Noor with a renewed sense of connection and purpose, helping her heal.

3: Zoya - Embracing New Beginnings

- **Challenge**: Zoya, a recent graduate, relocated to a new city for her first job, feeling lonely and disconnected from familiar surroundings.
- **RightQ Applied**: *"What new opportunities can I explore in this environment?"*
- **Outcome**: Zoya stepped out of her comfort zone by joining local cultural and professional groups. She also took up photography as a hobby, which allowed her to connect with others and turn her initial struggles into opportunities for personal and professional growth.

Faith as a Foundation for Strength

Faith provides an unwavering foundation of hope during life's toughest moments. For instance, Yasir, who faced a difficult financial crisis, found resilience through daily prayer and seeking support from his faith community. This practice not only helped him find clarity but also strengthened his trust in divine wisdom during uncertain times. Practices such as daily prayer, reflection on divine wisdom, or engaging in acts of community service provide a sense of grounding and resilience. For example, attending a prayer gathering or volunteering at a local charity can help reconnect you with a higher purpose and strengthen your resolve. By connecting with spiritual practices and reflecting on divine wisdom, we can find purpose in pain and turn trials into stepping stones for growth.

Faith-Inspired RightQs:

- *"What wisdom can I derive from this challenge?"*
- *"How can I demonstrate gratitude even during hardship?"*
- *"What actions will strengthen my trust in divine guidance?"*

Practical Exercise:

- Dedicate five minutes daily to reflect on the question: *"What has this challenge taught me about patience and trust in Divine Wisdom?"* Identify one specific way to apply this lesson in daily life, such as helping someone in need or adjusting your perspective on similar challenges. Reflect on your insights and align them with an actionable step, like showing kindness or improving how you approach difficulties.

Strategies for Building Resilience

1. **Faith-Based Visualization**
    - Visualize yourself overcoming challenges while trusting divine wisdom. Pair this with a RightQ: *"How can I align my actions today with the values of faith and perseverance?"*
2. **Collaborative Growth**
    - Seek community support by asking: *"Who in my circle can provide guidance or encouragement?"*

"What collective wisdom can I draw on to solve this problem?"

3. **Resilience Journaling**
    - Keep a record of past challenges, the RightQs you applied, and the results they led to. Reflect on this log to inspire future resilience.

Quotes for Reflection

- *"Adversity unveils the strength within us."*
- *"Faith transforms every obstacle into a path of growth."*
- *"With the right question, no challenge is insurmountable."*

Key Takeaways

- Faith and reflection transform challenges into growth opportunities.

- Resilience is strengthened through intentional action and community support.
- RightQs empower a mindset of gratitude, adaptability, and purpose.

Call to Action

Your Challenge, Your Growth:
Identify one current challenge and write down three RightQs to reframe it as an opportunity for growth. Reflect on how these questions can guide your actions and mindset. Commit to answering these questions over the next three days and take at least one actionable step based on your reflections.

Closing Reflection

Every challenge carries the seeds of growth and transformation. Through faith, intentional questioning, and a focus on possibilities, you can emerge stronger and more resilient.

"Every challenge holds a lesson; every question reveals the path forward."

CHAPTER 10: SUSTAINING GROWTH IN ADVERSITY

"Do not despair of the Mercy of Allah: for Allah forgives all sins: for He is Oft-Forgiving, Most Merciful." —Al-Quran 39:53

This verse speaks to the soul, offering profound reassurance that Allah's mercy is infinite and all-encompassing. It reminds us that no matter the depth of our struggles or mistakes, Allah's guidance and forgiveness are always within reach. This sets the foundation for the chapter, emphasizing resilience, trust, and hope as essential tools for navigating life's challenges.

Post-Crisis Transformation

Growth begins with the questions we ask after overcoming a challenge. Adversity, when met with reflection and intention, becomes a pivotal moment for personal transformation and renewed purpose.

Key RightQs for Post-Crisis Reflection:

- *"What inner strength have I discovered through this experience?"*

- *"How can I rebuild my life with greater intention and clarity?"*
- *"What steps can I take to strengthen my support systems for future challenges?"*

Maimoona's Story:
When a natural disaster devastated her hometown, Maimoona, a community leader, initially felt overwhelmed by the enormity of the loss. Instead of succumbing to despair, she asked herself:

"What role can I play in bringing hope back to my community?" This simple yet powerful question led her to organize a volunteer network that provided essential support and fostered unity. Maimoona's efforts transformed despair into a sense of purpose and resilience.

Avoiding Overthinking

Overthinking magnifies fear and uncertainty, often trapping us in endless cycles of doubt. Surrendering to Allah's will provides clarity and peace, allowing us to focus on what truly matters.

Practical Solution for Overthinking:

- Allocate a specific time each day (e.g., 15-30 minutes) to reflect on important subjects or decisions. Write down actionable steps or seek advice if needed.
- For the rest of the day, consciously release these thoughts by surrendering them to Divine Wisdom. Remind yourself: *"I have done my part; now I trust Divine Wisdom with the outcome."* Engage fully in life's blessings and live in the moment.

Faith-Based Practices:

- Begin your day with a short dua: **"My Lord, indeed I am in need of whatever good You would send down to me. "** – Quran 28:24
- Pair this with a RightQ: *"What step can I take today, trusting Divine Wisdom for the rest?"*

Overcoming Workplace Adversity

Workplace challenges, from interpersonal conflicts to high-pressure environments, are inevitable. These moments test our patience, resilience, and adaptability. By asking intentional RightQs, we can reframe these difficulties into opportunities for growth.

Example RightQs for Workplace Adversity:

- *"What is the root cause of this challenge, and how can I address it constructively?"*
- *"How can I align my actions with my values in this situation?"*
- *"What opportunities for growth does this adversity present?"*

This brief reflection creates a foundation for resolving workplace struggles with clarity and purpose.

Leveraging RightQs in Workplace Challenges

Workplace challenges, from conflicts to missed opportunities, can feel daunting. RightQs help shift focus from obstacles to solutions, empowering growth and collaboration.

Arshad's Story:
Arshad, a software engineer, felt frustrated when his ideas were dismissed in team meetings. Determined to improve, he asked himself: *"How can I present my ideas in a way that aligns with my team's goals?"* This question inspired him to adopt a collaborative approach, fostering mutual respect and gaining support. Over time, Arshad not only rebuilt his confidence but also enhanced team dynamics.

Reflection Prompts for Workplace Challenges:

- *"What communication skills can I improve to strengthen my professional relationships?"*
- *"How can I turn this challenge into an opportunity to grow my skills and confidence?"*

Practical Tools for Sustained Growth

Daily Reflection Log

- Keep a record of challenges, the RightQs applied, and the progress made.
  Example:
    - *Challenge*: Struggling with time management.
    - *RightQ*: "What is one task I can prioritize today to feel accomplished?"
    - *Outcome*: Improved focus and reduced stress.

Gratitude and Intention Journaling

- Each evening, write down three things you're grateful for and one intention for the next day.
  Example:
    - *Gratitude*: Supportive family, a productive day, and good health.
    - *Intention*: Practice patience and listen more attentively.

Community Engagement

- Share your experiences and seek support from others. Reflect on:
  "How can I contribute to my community while growing stronger myself?"

Quotes for Inspiration

- *"Trials teach us the strength we didn't know we had."*
- *"Faith turns every obstacle into a path of peace."*
- *"Growth is nurtured through challenges and sustained by trust in Divine Wisdom."*

Key Takeaways

- Growth after adversity is about rebuilding with clarity and intention.
- RightQs empower you to find solutions and foster resilience during difficult times.
- Surrendering to Divine Wisdom helps calm overthinking and brings peace.

Call to Action

Reflect on a recent or ongoing challenge. Write down three RightQs to reframe it positively. Take one intentional action today, trusting Divine guidance to light your path forward.

Closing Reflection

Adversity is not the end of your story—it is a chapter of growth and transformation. By trusting in Allah's mercy, embracing intentional questioning, and focusing on possibilities, you can navigate challenges with clarity, strength, and inner peace.

"Let your questions guide you, and your faith sustain you."

CHAPTER 11: LESSONS FROM GREAT THINKERS: A TIMELESS JOURNEY

Timeless Wisdom for Modern Living

Throughout history, great thinkers have shared profound insights that transcend time, guiding humanity toward clarity, wisdom, and purposeful living. From the poetic spirituality of Mawlānā Rūmī to the introspective reflections of Imam Ghazali, the metaphysical insights of Ibn Arabi, and the philosophical guidance of Mahatma Gandhi and Socrates, their timeless teachings illuminate pathways for growth and self-discovery.

Key Themes for Reflection

- The transformative power of self-awareness.
- Cultivating patience and resilience as tools for personal growth.
- Aligning actions with a higher purpose and universal values.

Insights from the Teachings of Great Thinkers

Imam Ja'far Sadiqؒ (702–765 CE):
Renowned for his profound debates and wisdom, Imam Ja'far Sadiqؒ highlighted the transformative power of reflection:
"A moment of reflection (Tafakkur) is worth more than seventy years of worship."

Key Reflection: How can I integrate moments of meaningful reflection into my daily routine to deepen my purpose and actions?

Imam Ghazaliؒ (1058–1111 CE):
A profound thinker in Islamic philosophy, Imam Ghazali emphasized self-purification and aligning actions with divine intent. In *The Alchemy of Happiness*, he wrote:
"The happiness of the heart comes when you detach from worldly distractions and turn toward the Creator."

Key Reflection: What worldly attachments can I release to create clarity and align with my higher purpose?

Ibn Arabiؒ (1165–1240 CE):
Ibn Arabi emphasized the interconnectedness of all creation and the importance of shifting perspectives. He taught:
"The real voyage of discovery consists not in seeking new landscapes, but in having new eyes."

Key Reflection: How can I view my current challenges as opportunities for growth and greater understanding?

Mawlānā Rūmīؒ (1207–1273 CE):
Mawlānā Rūmī's poetry celebrates divine love and the mysteries of existence. He encouraged embracing change with trust and curiosity:
"Try not to resist the changes that come your way. Instead, let life live through you."

Key Reflection: How can I embrace life's changes as pathways to uncovering my true potential?

Socrates (470/469–399 BCE):
Socrates, the father of Western philosophy, believed in the transformative power of introspection. He famously said:
"An unexamined life is not worth living."

Key Reflection: What can I learn about myself through intentional self-inquiry to live a more meaningful and purposeful life?

Ghalib (1797–1869):

The celebrated Urdu poet, Mirza Ghalib, delved into themes of existential reflection, resilience, and the quest for meaning amidst life's trials. Ghalib's words often highlight the beauty of introspection: **"The heart understands the joy of solitude, for it speaks to itself in silence."**

His poetry reminds us that self-awareness and the courage to confront our inner emotions are the keys to personal growth and understanding.

Key Reflection:

- How can I embrace moments of solitude to better understand my inner self and uncover clarity amidst life's noise?

Sir Muhammad Iqbal (1877–1938):

Known as the Poet of the East, Iqbal's philosophy centers on self-empowerment, faith, and the pursuit of one's divine potential. In his iconic work, *Bang-e-Dra,* Iqbal wrote:
"Elevate yourself so high that before fate decides, the Creator asks you what you desire."

This teaching emphasizes self-determination and aligning one's aspirations with a higher purpose, inspiring individuals to rise beyond limitations.

Key Reflection:

- How can I elevate my thoughts and actions to align with my highest potential and divine purpose?

Napoleon Hill (1883–1970 CE)

Napoleon Hill, the author of *Think and Grow Rich,* is one of the pioneers of modern self-help literature. He emphasized the importance of belief, persistence, and the power of a clear vision:
"Whatever the mind can conceive and believe, it can achieve."

Hill's philosophy encourages readers to set clear intentions, cultivate unwavering belief, and take consistent action toward their goals.

Key Reflection:

- What specific vision do I hold for my life, and how can I take consistent steps to turn it into reality?

Nikola Tesla (1856–1943 CE):

Nikola Tesla, the visionary inventor, believed in the interconnectedness of energy, thought, and the universe. Tesla famously said: **"If you want to find the secrets of the universe, think in terms of energy, frequency, and vibration."**

His teachings remind us to be mindful of our thoughts and their resonance with our actions, emphasizing that our energy shapes our reality.

Key Reflection:

- How can I align my thoughts and actions to resonate with the outcomes I wish to create in my life?

Mahatma Gandhi (1869–1948 CE):
Gandhiji emphasized aligning actions with values and cultivating strength through truth and nonviolence. He advised:
"Be the change that you wish to see in the world."

Key Reflection: What small but meaningful actions can I take today to embody the values I hold dear?

Neville Goddard (1905–1972 CE):

Neville Goddard, a proponent of the law of assumption, focused on the power of imagination and belief. He taught:
"Assume the feeling of your wish fulfilled, and act as if it is already yours."

This teaching encourages readers to live in alignment with their desires, using imagination as a tool to manifest positive outcomes.

Key Reflection:

- What would my life look like if my greatest goal were already achieved, and how can I embody that feeling today?

Reflection Prompts for Lifelong Learning

1. *"What lessons from these great thinkers resonate with my current journey?"*

2. *"How can I apply their wisdom to navigate my daily challenges?"*

3. *"What small, intentional changes can I make today to align more closely with their teachings?"*

Timeless RightQs for Reflection

To Reframe Challenges and Foster Growth:

1. *"What does this moment ask of me, and how can I respond with grace?"*

2. *"What strengths have I developed that I can apply to this challenge?"*

3. *"How can I align my actions today with my long-term purpose?"*

To Cultivate Creativity and Resilience:

4. *"What new perspective can I adopt to approach this problem with clarity and creativity?"*

5. *"What small, actionable step can I take to reframe this challenge as an opportunity?"*

To Deepen Self-Awareness:

6. *"What can I learn about myself through this experience?"*
7. *"How can I focus on what truly matters and filter out distractions?"*

Key Takeaways

- The wisdom of great thinkers inspires intentional living and self-awareness.
- Reflecting on timeless insights fosters clarity, resilience, and purpose.
- RightQs rooted in these teachings offer practical guidance for navigating modern complexities.

Call to Action

Choose one quote or teaching from this section and reflect on its relevance to your life. Write down a RightQ inspired by this wisdom and explore your answer through journaling or reflection.

Closing Reflection

The teachings of great thinkers remind us that personal growth is not a destination but a lifelong journey. By weaving their timeless insights into our daily lives and asking intentional questions, we can cultivate clarity, purpose, and inner peace.

"Let the beauty of what you love be what you do." – Mawlānā Rūmī◌ؒ

CHAPTER 12: ADVANCED TECHNIQUES FOR MASTERY

Taking RightQs to the Next Level

RightQs are transformative at every stage of life, but advanced techniques allow you to maximize their impact. Mastery lies in making your questions specific, actionable, and aligned with your values. With regular practice, you can uncover deeper insights and unlock your potential.

Mawlānā Rūmī reminds us:
"With life as short as a half-taken breath, don't plant anything but love."

Advanced RightQs help you focus on what truly matters, enabling you to take meaningful steps toward growth and fulfillment.

Customizing RightQs for Specific Life Stages

Life's challenges and opportunities vary across different stages, requiring intentional questions tailored to these unique contexts. RightQs offer a framework for clarity and action, enabling personal growth and adaptability at every phase of life.

RightQs for Early Adulthood (18-30):

- *"What skills can I develop to align with my long-term goals?"*
- *"How can I build habits today that will support my future aspirations?"*

RightQs for Midlife (30-50):

- *"How can I balance my responsibilities while nurturing my passions?"*
- *"What legacy do I want to create for my family and community?"*

RightQs for Later Life (50+):

- *"How can I use my experiences to guide and inspire others?"*
- *"What practices can I adopt to maintain mental and emotional well-being?"*

Making Layered Questioning Simple

Layered questioning helps you delve deeper into challenges or goals by asking a series of connected questions. Think of it as peeling layers of an onion—each question takes you closer to the core.

How to Use Layered Questions:

1. **Start with a broad question**:
    - *"What is my current goal?"*
2. **Narrow it down**:
    - *"What's stopping me from achieving it?"*
3. **Focus on action**:
    - *"What's the first step I can take today?"*

Practical Exercise:
Choose a situation you're struggling with. Write three related questions following this pattern. Reflect on your answers and write down one action you can take immediately.

Techniques for Enhanced Focus and Clarity

In a world full of distractions, staying focused and maintaining mental clarity are essential for effective decision-making and personal growth.

1. **Single-Tasking Over Multitasking**:
    - Focus on completing one task at a time.
    - RightQ: *"What is the most important thing I can accomplish right now?"*
2. **The Pomodoro Technique**:
    - Work in focused intervals (e.g., 25 minutes) followed by short breaks.
    - RightQ: *"What can I achieve in the next focused session?"*
3. **Mindful Transitions**:
    - Take a moment to pause and set intentions before switching tasks.
    - RightQ: *"How can I approach this new task with clarity and purpose?"*

Integrating Mindfulness Practices

Mindfulness enhances self-awareness, reduces stress, and promotes intentional living. Pairing mindfulness with RightQs amplifies its impact.

Simple Mindfulness Techniques:

- **Breath Awareness**: Focus on your breath for a few minutes.
  - RightQ: *"What can I release with each exhale, and what can I welcome with each inhale?"*
- **Body Scan**: Notice physical sensations from head to toe.
  - RightQ: *"What is my body telling me about my current state of mind?"*

Gratitude Pause:

- Reflect on three things you are grateful for.
  - RightQ: *"How can I honor these blessings through my actions today?"*

Real-Life Applications: Stories of Mastery

1. Early Adulthood:
Challenge: Dipti, a recent graduate, felt overwhelmed by career choices.
RightQs Applied:

- *"What steps can I take today to explore my interests and build my skills?"*
  Outcome: Dipti began volunteering and attending workshops, which helped her discover a passion for community development.

2. Midlife:
Challenge: Yusuf, a manager, struggled to balance work and family responsibilities.
RightQs Applied:

- *"What small changes can I make to create more meaningful connections at home?"*
  Outcome: Yusuf implemented family dinners and weekend activities, strengthening his relationships while maintaining professional success.

3. Later Life:
Challenge: Fahmida, a retired teacher, felt a loss of purpose after leaving her career.
RightQs Applied:

- *"How can I use my skills to benefit others in my community?"*
  Outcome: Fahmida started tutoring children in her neighborhood, finding fulfillment and creating a positive impact.

Quotes for Inspiration

- *"The questions you ask shape the life you build."*
- *"RightQs turn confusion into clarity and action into achievement."*
- *"Every breakthrough starts with a question that challenges the status quo."*

Key Takeaways for Chapter

- Layered questioning simplifies complex situations and leads to actionable insights.

- Customizing RightQs for specific areas of life ensures balanced growth and focus.
- Advanced techniques like visualization and micro-questions create immediate clarity and motivation.

Practical RightQs for Readers

Here's a list of ready-to-use RightQs to guide your journey:

- *"What is one thing I can improve today?"*
- *"How can I make this situation work in my favor?"*
- *"What lesson can I take from this challenge?"*
- *"How can I bring more joy into my daily life?"*
- *"What is a small step I can take toward my goal?"*

Closing Thought

Mastering RightQs isn't about asking perfect questions; it's about asking meaningful ones. Start small, stay consistent, and let your questions lead you to clarity and fulfillment.

"What you seek is seeking you—let your questions guide the way."

RightQs Workbook

A COMPREHENSIVE GUIDE FOR DAILY PRACTICE

This workbook is designed to help you apply RightQs consistently and effectively in your life. By combining structured reflection, practical tools, and interactive exercises, this guide empowers you to create meaningful growth and sustained progress.

Advanced Resource Kit for Sustained Progress

RightQs unlock clarity and purpose when used with intention. This workbook provides a structure to cultivate meaningful habits and integrate purposeful questioning into everyday actions.

Reflection Templates

1. Daily Reflection

Start and end your day with intentional questions that set the tone for focus and purpose.

Morning RightQs:

- "What is my primary focus today?"
- "How can I bring purpose to today's tasks?"

Evening RightQs:

- "What did I achieve today that I'm proud of?"
- "How can I improve tomorrow based on today's lessons?"

2. Weekly Reflection

Take time each week to review your progress and realign your actions with your goals.

Reflection Questions:

- "What wins did I celebrate this week?"
- "What challenges did I overcome, and how?"

Use these reflections to set actionable goals for the upcoming week.

---

3. Monthly and Yearly Reflection

Expand your reflections to achieve a broader perspective and plan for growth.

Monthly Reflection:

- "What was my biggest win this month?"
- "How have I grown through my challenges this month?"

Yearly Reflection:

- "What achievements am I most grateful for this year?"
- "What RightQs will guide me into the next year?"

---

4. Situational Reflection

Ask targeted questions during specific challenges or decisions for clarity and direction.

Situational RightQs:

- "What are my options, and which aligns best with my values?"
- "What potential outcomes do I foresee, and how can I prepare?"

Visualization Integration

Visualization enhances focus and helps you imagine desired outcomes. Use these tools to pair RightQs with purposeful imagery.

1. Vision Board Template

Create a visual representation of your goals and values.

RightQs to Guide Visualization:

- "What does success look like to me?"
- "What symbols or images inspire my progress?"

---

2. Layered Questioning Workflow (Visual Guide)

Refine insights step by step to clarify your goals.

Steps:

1. Start Broad: "What is my overarching goal?"
2. Focus: "What specific steps will bring me closer?"
3. Refine: "How can I make these steps impactful?"

---

3. Feedback Cycle Visualization

Diagram the process of action, reflection, adjustment, and growth.

Cycle: Action → Reflection → Adjustment → Growth

RightQs to Guide Reflection:

- "What worked well, and why?"
- "What adjustments can I make to improve results?"

Mini Case Studies for Practical Application

1. Overcoming Emotional Burnout

Scenario: Ravi, a software developer, faced constant burnout due to long hours and demanding projects. By reflecting on questions like "What boundaries can I set to protect my well-being?" and "How can I balance my work and personal life effectively?" Ravi started prioritizing his mental health by delegating tasks and scheduling regular breaks.

Outcome: Ravi regained his focus and energy, leading to enhanced productivity and job satisfaction.

2. Navigating Career Transitions

Scenario: Farah, a marketing strategist, struggled with adapting to a remote work environment as a new team lead. She asked herself, "What strengths can I leverage to manage my team effectively?" and "How can I foster trust in a virtual setting?" Farah implemented clear communication practices and virtual team-building activities.

Outcome: Farah successfully built a cohesive and motivated team, excelling in her leadership role.

---

3. Financial Crises

Scenario: Daniel, a single parent, faced mounting debts and uncertainty. He used RightQs like "What resources are available to help me rebuild financially?" and "How can I turn this challenge into a learning experience?" to create a budget, secure financial stability, and gain confidence.

Outcome: Daniel overcame his financial crisis with practical solutions and a renewed sense of security.

---

4. Workplace Conflict

Scenario: Anand, a project manager, faced communication gaps within his team during a critical project. He asked, "What steps can I take to ensure transparency and collaboration?" and "How can I mediate conflicts constructively?" Anand initiated weekly check-ins and facilitated open discussions.

Outcome: Anand improved team communication, leading to smoother workflows and timely project delivery.

Outcome: Anand developed a more harmonious work environment through open communication.

RightQs to Purify the Soul from Negative Traits

Transforming Lust into Contentment:

1. *"How can I redirect my desires toward what truly benefits my soul?"*
2. *"What actions will bring me closer to inner peace?"*
3. *"Why is self-restraint a source of strength?"*
4. *"What virtues can I cultivate to elevate my intentions?"*

Transforming Greed into Generosity:

1. *"What blessings in my life can I share with others?"*
2. *"How does giving enrich my soul?"*
3. *"Why is contentment the key to lasting happiness?"*
4. *"What can I do today to help someone in need?"*

Transforming Jealousy into Admiration:

1. *"What lessons can I learn from the success of others?"*
2. *"How can I use my unique abilities to achieve my goals?"*
3. *"Why is gratitude a remedy for envy?"*
4. *"What qualities in others inspire me to improve myself?"*

Transforming Arrogance into Humility:

1. *"How can I acknowledge the contributions of others in my success?"*
2. *"Why is humility essential for personal growth?"*
3. *"What actions can I take to serve others without seeking recognition?"*
4. *"What reminders help me stay grounded and grateful?"*

Transforming Anger into Patience:

1. *"What wisdom can I gain by pausing before I react?"*
2. *"How can I approach this situation with compassion?"*

3. *"Why is patience a sign of strength?"*
4. *"What alternative responses can lead to peace?"*

Transforming Laziness into Diligence:

1. *"What small step can I take right now to start moving forward?"*
2. *"Why is effort a gift to myself and those around me?"*
3. *"What motivates me to honor my time and energy?"*
4. *"How does persistence lead to lasting rewards?"*

Transforming Envy into Gratitude:

1. *"What blessings in my life deserve my attention and thanks?"*
2. *"How can I celebrate the achievements of others while pursuing my own goals?"*
3. *"Why is contentment a path to inner joy?"*
4. *"What strengths within me can I nurture to create my success?"*

Interactive Exercises

Engaging with RightQs through actionable exercises helps to solidify their transformative potential in daily life. These exercises are designed to integrate questioning into various aspects of your routine, fostering intentionality and growth.

1. The Morning Alignment Ritual

Start your day with clarity and focus by dedicating five minutes each morning to intentional questioning.

RightQs:

- "What is one meaningful action I can take today to align with my values?"
- "What opportunities might arise today, and how can I embrace them?"

Action: Write down your response and revisit it in the evening to reflect on your progress.

---

2. Reframing Negative Thoughts

Overcome limiting beliefs by turning them into empowering questions.

RightQs:

- Negative: "Why do things always go wrong for me?"
- Reframed: "What lesson can I learn from this challenge?"

Action: Create a two-column table in your journal. In the left column, list recurring negative thoughts. In the right, reframe each into a constructive RightQ.

---

3. Gratitude and Growth Journal

Enhance mindfulness and resilience by pairing gratitude with actionable insights.

RightQs:

- "What am I most grateful for today?"
- "How can I use this gratitude to inspire my actions tomorrow?"

Action: Write three things you are grateful for each evening, along with one question that will guide your actions the next day.

---

4. The Five-Minute Reflection

At the end of a busy day, carve out five minutes to review and recalibrate.

RightQs:

- "What did I achieve today that I'm proud of?"
- "What small step can I take tomorrow to continue this momentum?"

Action: Use a habit tracker to note your reflection streak, motivating consistency.

---

5. Vision Board Questioning

Pair visualizations with RightQs to keep your goals front and center.

RightQs:

- "What small action today will bring me closer to this vision?"
- "What resources or skills do I need to achieve this goal?"

Action: Create or update a vision board, ensuring each image aligns with a question. Place it somewhere visible to inspire daily action.

Engagement

Join the Word of Wisdom Community:

- Visit www.wordofwisdom.in for exclusive content and support.

Key Takeaways

- Structured reflections amplify the impact of RightQs.
- Visualization tools turn goals into actionable plans.
- Real-life examples highlight the transformative power of intentional questioning.

Closing Thought

This workbook serves as your guide to making RightQs a cornerstone of personal growth. By reflecting, acting, and adjusting, you'll navigate life's challenges with clarity, confidence, and resilience.

"The questions you ask shape the path you take."

CONCLUSION: A JOURNEY OF LIFELONG DISCOVERY

Reflecting on the Journey

Growth begins with reflection—a deliberate pause to assess where you've been and where you're headed. Reflection turns past challenges into stepping stones, offering clarity and purpose for the road ahead.

Mawlānā Rūmī reminds us:
"Be like a lamp, or a lifeboat, or a ladder. Help someone's soul heal."

By embracing intentional questioning, you illuminate your path and inspire others to embark on their own transformative journeys.

Reflection Prompts:

- *"What lessons have I learned from my recent challenges?"*
- *"How have my actions aligned with my values over the past month?"*

- *"What strengths have I cultivated through difficult times?"*

The Transformative Power of RightQs

RightQs are not just tools—they are a way of life. Each question you ask holds the potential to:

- Transform your perspective.
- Reveal hidden opportunities.
- Strengthen your resilience.
- Deepen your connection to your true self.

Intentional questioning bridges the gap between aspiration and action, guiding you toward a fulfilling and intentional life.

Sustaining Growth Through Reflection

Reflection is the anchor that keeps you aligned with your goals and adaptable to life's changes. Consistent reflection transforms growth from a momentary breakthrough into a lifelong habit.

Practical Tips for Consistency:

1. **Daily Check-In**: Spend five minutes each evening reviewing the day's progress. Ask:
   - *"What went well today?"*
   - *"What can I improve tomorrow?"*
2. **Weekly Reviews**: Dedicate time each weekend to assess successes and challenges. Ask:
   - *"What steps brought me closer to my goals?"*
   - *"What adjustments can I make for next week?"*
3. **Monthly Reflection**: Take a broader view to evaluate progress and refine long-term aspirations.

Faith-Aligned Insight:

Growth is a journey guided by divine wisdom and mercy. Approach each reflection with gratitude for progress and patience for areas that are still evolving.

Inspiring the World Around You

Your growth has the power to inspire others. When you embody clarity, purpose, and resilience, you spark curiosity and motivation in those around you. Thoughtful questions can ignite meaningful conversations and collective growth.

Reflection Prompts:

- *"How can I use what I've learned to contribute to the well-being of others?"*
- *"What legacy of questions and actions do I want to leave behind?"*

Strengthening Community Connections

Growth flourishes when shared. Engaging with a community fosters collective progress and amplifies the impact of your journey.

Ways to Connect:

1. **Word of Wisdom Platform**:
   Visit www.wordofwisdom.in to:
   - Access curated content on personal growth.

- Participate in discussions to share insights and RightQs.
- Utilize exclusive tools like journaling templates and habit trackers.

2. **Other Platforms**:
   - **Meetup.com**: Join groups focused on mindfulness and self-improvement.
   - **LinkedIn Groups**: Engage with communities encouraging intentional living.
   - **Reddit Communities**: Share insights on forums like r/selfimprovement or r/wordsofwisdom_in

Actionable Steps:

- Form accountability groups to practice RightQs collectively.
- Host events or meet-ups to exchange insights and build meaningful connections.

Reflection Prompts for Community Building:

- *"How can I contribute to a community that fosters mutual growth?"*
- *"What role can I play in nurturing intentional living among others?"*

Final Reflections and Encouragement

As you step into the next chapter of your life, remember that every question you ask holds the power to shape your future. Make them count.

Approach each day with gratitude, curiosity, and the courage to ask purposeful questions.

Reflective Prompts for Readers:

- *"What question will I ask myself today to guide my actions?"*
- *"How can I use the lessons in this book to inspire others?"*
- *"What step can I take right now to live intentionally?"*

Universal Takeaway:
"The journey of growth begins with a single question. Let your questions lead you to clarity, purpose, and fulfillment."

Your transformation through RightQs extends beyond personal growth—it creates ripples that can positively impact your family, community, and workplace.

Parting Thought:

"The questions we ask determine the life we lead. Let your questions be intentional, your actions meaningful, and your life a reflection of your highest values."

May this journey of discovery bring you clarity, fulfillment, and unwavering purpose. Let the RightQs you ask guide you toward becoming your best self and inspiring others to do the same.

---

www.ingramcontent.com/pod-product-compliance
Lightning Source LLC
Chambersburg PA
CBHW062141160726
48282CB00027B/892
9789334217629